I0406987

THE ULTIMATE GUIDE TO

BUILDING A PASSIVE INCOME EMPIRE

OLADEJO ANUOLUWAPO

The Ultimate Guide to Building a Passive

Income Empire

Written By:

Oladejo Anuoluwapo

Table of Contents

Introduction

Chapter 1: Understanding Passive Income - The Foundation of Wealth Building

Chapter 2: Setting the Foundation for Your Passive Income Empire

Chapter 3: Investing for Passive Income - Building a Strong Financial Foundation

Chapter 4: Building Passive Income Streams - Leveraging Your Skills and Assets

Chapter 5: Passive Income through Real Estate - Building a Solid Foundation

Chapter 6: The Power of Dividends - Building Wealth One Payout at a Time

Chapter 7: Online Business Ventures - Unleashing the Digital Potential

Chapter 8: Peer-to-Peer Lending - A Unique Approach to Passive Income

Chapter 9: Realizing the Potential of Dividend Growth Investing

Chapter 10: The Art of Rental Properties - Unlocking Real Estate Passive

Conclusion

Introduction: The Ultimate Guide to Building a Passive Income Empire

Welcome to "The Ultimate Guide to Building a Passive Income Empire." In the pursuit of financial freedom and security, many individuals aspire to create income streams that require minimal day-to-day effort and allow them to enjoy life on their own terms. This guide is your roadmap to achieving that goal.

The concept of a passive income empire represents the epitome of financial independence. It's about establishing diverse and sustainable sources of income that continue to flow in, even when you're not actively working. Whether you dream of traveling the world, spending more time with your loved ones, or simply having the freedom to pursue your passions without worrying about finances, passive income can make it a reality.

This guide is designed to be your comprehensive resource, covering a wide range of passive income strategies and providing the knowledge and tools you need to create, grow, and manage your passive income empire. We'll explore proven techniques and cutting-edge opportunities, from traditional investments like real estate and dividend stocks to innovative online business ventures, peer-to-peer lending, and much more.

Each chapter will take you on a journey through a different passive income avenue, offering insights, strategies, and practical advice to help you navigate the path to financial independence. Whether you're a novice looking to start your passive income journey or an experienced investor seeking to diversify your income sources, this guide has something valuable to offer.

Building a passive income empire is not just about amassing wealth; it's about gaining control over your time, reducing financial stress, and creating a future where you can live life on your own terms. So, let's embark on this journey together, exploring the endless possibilities of passive income and taking steps towards your brighter, more financially secure future. Your path to financial independence begins here.

Chapter 1

Understanding Passive Income - The Foundation of Wealth Building

Introduction

Welcome to "The Ultimate Guide to Building a Passive Income Empire." In this chapter, we will lay the foundation for your journey towards financial independence and wealth accumulation through passive income. You'll discover the fundamental concepts of passive income, why it's essential, and how it can transform your financial future.

What is Passive Income?

Passive income is money earned with minimal effort or active involvement on your part. It's the opposite of trading your time for money, which is the typical model of traditional employment. Instead of being paid for each hour you work, passive income allows you to generate revenue continuously, whether you're working, sleeping, or enjoying your life to the fullest.

Imagine waking up in the morning and finding that you've earned money while you slept – that's the power of passive income. It provides financial security, freedom, and the potential to build wealth far beyond what a 9-to-5 job can offer.

Why Build a Passive Income Empire?

Building a passive income empire is not just a financial aspiration; it's a pathway to a more fulfilling and liberated life. Here are some compelling reasons why you should embark on this journey:

1. Financial Security

Passive income acts as a safety net, providing you with a reliable stream of money even in uncertain times. It cushions you against job loss, economic downturns, and unexpected expenses.

2. Freedom and Flexibility

Passive income empowers you to take control of your time. You're no longer chained to a desk or a rigid work schedule. You can choose when and where you work, or even take extended breaks without worrying about lost income.

3. Wealth Accumulation

Passive income isn't just about meeting your basic needs; it's a powerful tool for accumulating wealth. As your income streams grow, so does your net worth. Over time, this can lead to financial abundance and the ability to achieve your life's goals.

4. Pursue Your Passions

When you're not bound by a 9-to-5 job, you have the freedom to pursue your passions and interests. Whether it's traveling, starting a side business, or dedicating more time to your family, passive income allows you to do what matters most to you.

5. Leave a Legacy

With a well-established passive income empire, you can create a lasting legacy for your loved ones. You'll have the means to provide for future generations and support causes that are close to your heart.

The Passive Income Mindset

Before diving into the practical strategies and techniques for building passive income streams, it's crucial to adopt the right mindset. Here are some key principles to keep in mind:

1. Patience and Persistence

Building a passive income empire takes time and effort. You won't see immediate results, but with persistence, your income will grow exponentially.

2. Continuous Learning

The world of passive income is ever-evolving. Stay curious and open to new opportunities. Be willing to learn and adapt to changes in the market.

3. Risk Management

Not all passive income opportunities are risk-free. It's essential to assess and manage risks effectively to protect your financial well-being.

4. Diversification

Don't put all your eggs in one basket. Diversify your passive income streams to spread risk and increase stability.

In the chapters that follow, we'll explore various passive income strategies, including investments, online businesses, real estate, and more. Each strategy comes with its own set of opportunities and challenges, and you'll learn how to navigate them all.

Are you ready to embark on this exciting journey toward financial freedom? It begins with a deep understanding of passive income, its benefits, and the right mindset. So, let's dive in and explore the world of building a passive income empire together.

Chapter 2:

Setting the Foundation for Your Passive Income Empire

Introduction

In the previous chapter, you learned about the concept of passive income and why it's essential for your financial well-being and freedom. Now, it's time to set the foundation for your passive income empire. This chapter will guide you through the crucial steps of assessing your financial goals, creating a passive income strategy, and building a financial safety net.

Assessing Your Financial Goals

Before you can embark on your journey to building a passive income empire, it's essential to have clear and well-defined financial goals. Your goals will serve as your roadmap, helping you determine how much passive income you need and what strategies are best suited to your needs. Here's how to get started:

1. Short-Term vs. Long-Term Goals

Begin by distinguishing between your short-term and long-term financial goals. Short-term goals might include paying off debts, building an emergency fund, or saving for a vacation. Long-term goals may involve retirement planning, buying a home, or achieving financial independence.

2. Quantify Your Goals

For each financial goal, quantify it in specific, measurable terms. Instead of a vague goal like "save more money," set a precise target, such as "save $10,000 for a down payment on a house within three years."

3. Prioritize Your Goals

Not all goals are equally important. Prioritize them based on their significance and urgency. This will help you focus your efforts on the most critical objectives.

4. Timeframes

Determine the timeframes for achieving each goal. Knowing when you want to reach your goals will help you create a realistic passive income strategy.

5. Consider Inflation and Lifestyle Changes

Account for inflation and potential changes in your lifestyle. What may be enough passive income today might not suffice in the future due to rising costs or evolving priorities.

6. Seek Professional Guidance

If you're unsure about setting financial goals or need assistance in quantifying them, consider consulting a financial advisor. They can provide valuable insights and help you create a tailored plan.

Creating a Passive Income Strategy

With your financial goals in mind, it's time to craft a passive income strategy. This strategy will guide your decisions and actions as you work toward building your empire.

1. Identify Income Sources

Start by identifying potential sources of passive income. These can include:

- **Investments**: Stocks, bonds, real estate, and other assets that generate income.

- **Business Ventures**: Online businesses, rental properties, or partnerships.

- **Intellectual Property**: Books, courses, music, or art that can be licensed or sold.

- **Dividend Stocks**: Shares in companies that distribute a portion of their profits to shareholders.

- **Peer-to-Peer Lending**: Earning interest by lending money to individuals or businesses.

2. Set Income Targets

For each income source, establish income targets based on your financial goals. Determine how much money you need to generate from each source to achieve your objectives.

3. Risk Assessment

Evaluate the risks associated with each income source. Different strategies come with varying levels of risk, and it's crucial to align your risk tolerance with your chosen methods.

4. Diversification

Consider diversifying your income sources to spread risk. Relying solely on one income stream can be risky; having multiple streams provides stability.

5. Asset Allocation

In investment-related income sources, decide how you'll allocate your assets. This may involve choosing a mix of stocks, bonds, and other investments to balance risk and reward.

6. Time Commitment

Assess the time commitment required for each income source. Some passive income streams may demand more initial effort than others but require minimal ongoing maintenance.

Building a Financial Safety Net

While pursuing passive income, it's essential to build a financial safety net to protect yourself and your investments. Here are steps to consider:

1. Emergency Fund

Maintain an emergency fund with at least three to six months' worth of living expenses. This fund will cover unexpected costs without derailing your passive income goals.

2. Insurance

Review your insurance coverage, including health, disability, life, and property insurance. Adequate coverage ensures you're financially protected in case of unforeseen events.

3. Debt Management

Address high-interest debts like credit cards as a priority. Reducing debt burdens will free up more of your income for passive investments.

4. Legal and Tax Planning

Consult with legal and tax professionals to ensure your assets and income sources are structured efficiently and comply with applicable laws.

By setting clear goals, creating a strategic plan, and establishing a financial safety net, you're laying a solid foundation for your passive income empire. In the upcoming chapters, we'll delve into specific passive income strategies, providing you with actionable steps to turn your goals into reality. Your journey to financial freedom has begun.

Chapter 3:

Investing for Passive Income - Building a Strong Financial Foundation

Introduction

In the previous chapters, you gained an understanding of passive income and laid the groundwork for your journey towards financial independence. Now, it's time to dive into one of the most powerful ways to generate passive income: **investing**. This chapter will explore various investment avenues and strategies to help you build a strong financial foundation for your passive income empire.

The Power of Investments

Investing is the process of allocating your money into assets or ventures with the expectation of generating income or achieving capital appreciation over time. When it comes to building a passive income empire, investments are a cornerstone. Here's why:

1. Compounding Returns

Investments can generate **compounding returns**. This means that your earnings generate additional earnings over time, snowballing your wealth. The longer you invest, the more significant the compounding effect.

2. Diverse Income Streams

Different types of investments offer various income streams, such as dividends, interest, rental income, and capital gains. By diversifying your investments, you can create multiple passive income sources.

3. Wealth Preservation

Investments can act as a hedge against inflation. As the value of money decreases due to inflation, your investments can potentially grow in value, preserving your wealth.

4. Tax Benefits

Many investments offer tax advantages, such as tax-deferred growth or preferential tax rates on certain types of income. These benefits can optimize your after-tax returns.

Types of Investments

There is a multitude of investment opportunities available, each with its own risk-reward profile. Here are some of the most common types of investments for generating passive income:

1. **Stock Market Investments**

- **Dividend Stocks**: Invest in shares of companies that distribute a portion of their profits to shareholders in the form of dividends.

- **Growth Stocks**: Focus on stocks with high growth potential, which may not provide immediate income but can yield significant capital gains over time.

2. Real Estate Investments

- **Rental Properties**: Purchase residential or commercial properties and earn rental income from tenants.

- **Real Estate Investment Trusts (REITs)**: Invest in publicly traded companies that own and manage income-producing real estate properties.

- **Crowdfunding Real Estate**: Participate in real estate investment opportunities through crowdfunding platforms.

3. Bonds

- **Corporate Bonds**: Lend money to corporations in exchange for regular interest payments and the return of the principal amount at maturity.

- **Government Bonds**: Invest in bonds issued by governments, which are generally considered lower risk than corporate bonds.

4. Peer-to-Peer (P2P) Lending

- Participate in online lending platforms where you lend money to individuals or small businesses in exchange for interest payments.

5. Creating and Selling Digital Products

- Develop digital products such as ebooks, online courses, or software and sell them online. These products can provide recurring income with minimal ongoing effort.

Building Your Investment Portfolio

Building a well-diversified investment portfolio is key to managing risk and optimizing returns. Here are steps to consider:

1. Define Your Investment Goals

- What is the purpose of your investments? Are you primarily seeking income or long-term growth? Your goals will influence your investment choices.

2. Assess Your Risk Tolerance

- Understand your risk tolerance, which is the level of risk you can comfortably handle. Risk tolerance varies from person to person, and it's essential to align your investments with your comfort level.

3. Asset Allocation

- Determine how you'll allocate your investments among different asset classes, such as stocks, bonds, real estate, and alternative investments.

4. Diversification

- Diversify your investments within each asset class to spread risk. Avoid putting all your money into a single investment.

5. Regular Monitoring

- Periodically review your investment portfolio and make adjustments as needed. Rebalancing your portfolio ensures it aligns with your goals and risk tolerance.

6. Consider Tax Efficiency

- Be mindful of the tax implications of your investments. Utilize tax-advantaged accounts when appropriate, and consider tax-efficient investment strategies.

The Importance of Patience

One of the essential qualities of a successful investor is **patience**. Building a passive income empire through investments takes time. Market fluctuations are normal, but over the long term, investments tend to appreciate in value and provide steady income.

Conclusion

Investing for passive income is a powerful way to build a strong financial foundation for your empire. By understanding the various types of investments, setting clear goals, and managing risk through diversification, you can create a portfolio that generates income while you sleep. In the next chapters, we'll explore other passive income strategies, so you can continue to expand and fortify your empire.

Chapter 4:

Building Passive Income Streams - Leveraging Your Skills and Assets

Introduction

In the journey to build your passive income empire, you've learned about the power of investments. Now, we'll explore another avenue that doesn't require large capital upfront: **creating passive income streams**. In this chapter, you'll discover how to leverage your skills, knowledge, and existing assets to generate income while reducing the need for significant financial investments.

The Versatility of Passive Income Streams

While investments play a crucial role in building wealth passively, creating income streams offers versatility and agility. You can start small, gradually scale up, and adapt to changing circumstances. Here's why creating income streams is an essential part of your passive income strategy:

1. Low Capital Requirements

Many passive income streams require minimal upfront investment, making them accessible to a broader range of individuals.

2. Diverse Opportunities

There are numerous ways to create passive income streams, from online businesses to content creation, intellectual property, and more. This diversity allows you to choose the methods that align with your interests and expertise.

3. Scalability

As your passive income streams grow, you have the flexibility to scale them up to generate even more income over time.

4. Geographic Independence

Creating income streams often provides location independence, allowing you to work from anywhere with an internet connection.

Passive Income Streams through Online Business Ventures

The digital age has opened up countless opportunities to build passive income streams online. Here are some popular options:

1. **Blogging and Affiliate Marketing**

- Start a blog on a niche topic you're passionate about.

- Monetize it by promoting affiliate products or services.

- Over time, your blog can attract a steady stream of visitors and generate affiliate income.

2. YouTube and Video Content

- Create a YouTube channel around your interests or expertise.

- Earn revenue through ads, sponsorships, and affiliate marketing as your channel grows in popularity.

3. Podcasting

- Launch a podcast on a subject you're knowledgeable about.

- Monetize it through sponsorships, merchandise sales, or listener donations.

4. Ebook Publishing

- Write and publish ebooks on platforms like Amazon Kindle.

- Ebooks can provide passive income as long as they continue to sell.

5. Membership Sites and Subscription Services

- Create a membership site offering premium content or a community forum.

- Charge a monthly or annual fee for access.

6. Software as a Service (SaaS)

- Develop a software application or tool that solves a specific problem.

- Charge users on a subscription basis.

Building Your Online Presence

Regardless of the online business venture you choose, building your online presence is critical. Here's how to get started:

1. Identify Your Niche

- Choose a niche or topic you're passionate about and have expertise in. A well-defined niche will help you stand out in a crowded online landscape.

2. Create High-Quality Content

- Consistently produce valuable content that resonates with your target audience. Whether it's blog posts, videos, podcasts, or ebooks, quality matters.

3. SEO and Marketing

- Learn about search engine optimization (SEO) to improve your content's visibility in search engines.

- Promote your content through social media, email marketing, and other channels.

4. Monetization Strategies

- Implement monetization strategies that fit your chosen platform and audience. For example, affiliate marketing, sponsorships, or premium content.

Passive Income through Intellectual Property

Intellectual property (IP) can be a lucrative source of passive income. If you possess expertise in a particular field, you can create and sell IP assets, such as:

1. Online Courses

- Develop and sell online courses on platforms like Udemy or Teachable.

2. Books and Guides

- Write and publish books, guides, or whitepapers related to your expertise.

3. Licensing

- License your intellectual property, such as software, patents, or artwork, to others for a fee.

Leveraging Existing Assets

In addition to creating digital assets, you can leverage existing resources for passive income:

1. **Rent Out Property**

- If you own real estate, consider renting out part of your property as an Airbnb host or long-term rental.

2. Storage Space

- If you have extra storage space, rent it out to individuals or businesses in need of storage solutions.

3. Photography and Art

- If you're a photographer or artist, sell your work online through platforms like Shutterstock or Etsy.

4. Unused Items

- Declutter your home and sell unused items through online marketplaces like eBay or Craigslist.

Conclusion

Building passive income streams through online business ventures, intellectual property, and leveraging existing assets empowers you to generate income with creativity, expertise, and minimal upfront investment. The key is to find opportunities that align with your passions and skills, and to nurture these streams over time. In the next chapters, we'll explore more ways to diversify your passive income portfolio and secure your financial future. Your empire is taking shape, one stream at a time.

Chapter 5:

Passive Income through Real Estate - Building a Solid Foundation

Introduction

Real estate has long been recognized as one of the most reliable ways to generate passive income and build wealth over time. In this chapter, we will delve into the world of **real estate investments** as a powerful strategy to further develop your passive income empire. Whether you're interested in rental properties, real estate investment trusts (REITs), or crowdfunding real estate, this chapter will guide you through the process of getting started and reaping the rewards of real estate passive income.

The Allure of Real Estate for Passive Income

Real estate offers unique advantages for passive income seekers:

1. **Steady Cash Flow**: Rental properties can provide a consistent stream of rental income, creating reliable cash flow.

2. **Appreciation**: Real estate properties tend to appreciate in value over time, potentially increasing your net worth.

3. **Tax Benefits**: Real estate investments come with various tax advantages, such as depreciation deductions and tax-advantaged accounts like 1031 exchanges.

4. **Leverage**: You can use financing to purchase real estate properties, allowing you to control larger assets with a smaller initial investment.

5. **Portfolio Diversification**: Real estate investments can diversify your overall investment portfolio, reducing risk.

Types of Real Estate Investments

There are several avenues for investing in real estate, each with its own risk-reward profile and income potential:

1. **Rental Properties**

- Purchase residential or commercial properties and generate income by renting them out to tenants.

- Rental income can provide a consistent monthly cash flow.

2. **Real Estate Investment Trusts (REITs)**

- Invest in publicly traded companies that own, operate, or finance income-producing real estate properties.

- REITs typically distribute at least 90% of their taxable income to shareholders, making them an attractive income option.

3. **Crowdfunding Real Estate**

- Participate in real estate investment opportunities through online crowdfunding platforms.

- Invest alongside other individuals in larger real estate projects, such as apartment complexes or commercial buildings.

Getting Started with Rental Properties

If you're interested in rental properties as a source of passive income, here are the essential steps to consider:

1. Market Research

- Research local real estate markets to identify areas with high rental demand and potential for appreciation.

2. Property Selection

- Choose the type of property you want to invest in, such as single-family homes, multi-family units, or commercial properties.

3. Financing

- Secure financing for your property, either through a mortgage or alternative financing options.

4. Property Management

- Decide whether you will manage the property yourself or hire a property management company to handle tenant relations, maintenance, and rent collection.

5. Tenant Screening

- Implement a thorough tenant screening process to find reliable tenants who will pay rent on time and take care of the property.

6. Property Maintenance

- Regularly maintain the property to keep it in good condition, which helps retain tenants and property value.

7. Legal and Tax Considerations

- Consult with legal and tax professionals to ensure you comply with local laws and take advantage of tax deductions and benefits.

Real Estate Investment Trusts (REITs)

Investing in REITs provides a way to access the real estate market without owning physical properties. Here's how to get started with REITs:

1. Choose a REIT Type

- REITs come in various forms, including equity REITs, mortgage REITs, and hybrid REITs. Determine which type aligns with your investment goals.

2. Select REITs

- Research and choose specific REITs to invest in. Look at their track record, dividend history, and property portfolio.

3. Open an Investment Account

- Open a brokerage or investment account to buy shares of REITs.

4. Regular Investment

- Consider setting up regular investments to accumulate shares over time.

5. Monitor Performance

- Keep track of your REIT investments' performance and adjust your portfolio as needed.

Crowdfunding Real Estate

Crowdfunding real estate platforms provide opportunities to invest in real estate projects alongside other investors. Here's how to get started:

1. Research Platforms

- Research crowdfunding platforms to find one that aligns with your investment goals and risk tolerance.

2. Diversify

- Diversify your investments by spreading your funds across multiple real estate projects.

3. Due Diligence

- Conduct thorough due diligence on the projects you're interested in, including reviewing project details, financials, and the track record of the project sponsor.

4. Invest and Monitor

- Invest in projects that meet your criteria and monitor their progress.

Conclusion

Real estate investments can be a cornerstone of your passive income empire, offering reliable cash flow, potential for appreciation, and tax advantages. Whether you choose rental properties, REITs, or crowdfunding real estate, it's crucial to conduct thorough research, understand the risks, and develop a strategy that aligns with your financial goals. In the next chapters, we'll explore additional passive income strategies, helping you diversify and strengthen your empire. Your journey to financial independence is well underway.

Chapter 6:

The Power of Dividends - Building Wealth One Payout at a Time

Introduction

Dividend income is one of the most time-tested and reliable ways to build a passive income empire. In this chapter, we will explore the world of **dividend investing** and how it can play a crucial role in your journey towards financial independence. You'll learn about the benefits of dividend stocks, how to build a dividend portfolio, and strategies for maximizing your dividend income.

Understanding Dividend Income

Dividend income is the money paid to shareholders by companies as a portion of their profits. Unlike capital gains, which result from selling an asset for a profit, dividends are a distribution of earnings to shareholders. Here's why dividend income is a powerful tool for building wealth:

1. **Steady Income**

- Dividends provide a regular stream of income, typically paid quarterly or annually.

2. **Income Growth**

- Many companies increase their dividends over time, leading to income growth that outpaces inflation.

3. Portfolio Stability

- Dividend-paying stocks often exhibit greater stability during market downturns, making them a valuable addition to a diversified portfolio.

4. Compounding Effect

- Reinvesting dividends allows you to take advantage of the compounding effect, where your earnings generate additional earnings.

Building a Dividend Portfolio

Creating a dividend portfolio involves carefully selecting dividend-paying stocks and managing your investments for long-term growth. Here are the steps to get started:

1. Define Your Investment Goals

- Determine your financial objectives, such as the amount of dividend income you want to generate and your desired timeline.

2. Research Dividend Stocks

- Identify companies known for their consistent dividend payments. Look for those with a history of increasing dividends.

3. Diversify Your Portfolio

- Avoid putting all your money into a single stock or sector. Diversify across different industries to spread risk.

4. Evaluate Dividend Yield and Growth

- Consider stocks with a balance between a reasonable dividend yield (the annual dividend income as a percentage of the stock's price) and a history of dividend growth.

5. Assess Company Fundamentals

- Examine the financial health of the companies you're interested in, including their earnings, debt levels, and business prospects.

6. Reinvest Dividends

- Consider enrolling in a dividend reinvestment plan (DRIP) to reinvest your dividends automatically.

7. Regular Monitoring

- Continuously monitor your dividend portfolio to ensure it aligns with your goals and adjust as needed.

Strategies for Maximizing Dividend Income

To maximize your dividend income, consider the following strategies:

1. Dividend Aristocrats and Champions

- These are companies with a history of consistently increasing dividends for 25 or more years. They are often reliable choices for long-term dividend growth.

2. High Dividend Yield Stocks

- While high-yield stocks offer more immediate income, exercise caution, as very high yields may signal financial distress. Balance yield with sustainability.

3. Sector and Industry Focus

- Diversify your dividend portfolio across various sectors to reduce risk. Some sectors, like utilities and consumer staples, are known for stable dividends.

4. Dividend ETFs

- Consider dividend-focused exchange-traded funds (ETFs) that offer diversification and professional management.

5. Tax-Efficient Investing

- Utilize tax-advantaged accounts like IRAs or 401(k)s to minimize the tax impact of your dividend income.

6. International Dividend Stocks

- Explore international dividend-paying stocks to diversify your income sources and potentially access higher yields.

7. Options Strategies

- Advanced investors can use options strategies to enhance their dividend income, such as covered call writing.

Risks and Considerations

While dividend investing offers numerous benefits, it's essential to be aware of potential risks:

1. Market Volatility

- Dividend stocks can still be subject to market fluctuations. Be prepared for occasional price declines.

2. Dividend Cuts

- Companies may reduce or eliminate dividends during challenging economic times. Diversification can mitigate this risk.

3. Interest Rate Changes

- Rising interest rates can make dividend stocks less attractive compared to fixed-income investments.

4. Company-Specific Risks

- Analyze individual companies for specific risks that may affect their ability to pay dividends.

Conclusion

Dividend income investing is a powerful strategy to build a passive income empire. It offers a reliable and growing income stream, portfolio stability, and the potential for significant wealth accumulation over time. By carefully selecting dividend stocks, diversifying your portfolio, and employing smart investment strategies, you can harness the power of dividends to achieve your financial goals. In the next chapters, we'll explore more passive income strategies to help you diversify and strengthen your empire. Your journey to financial independence continues with the wisdom of dividend investing.

<h1 style="text-align:center">Chapter 7:</h1>

<h2 style="text-align:center">Online Business Ventures - Unleashing the Digital Potential</h2>

Introduction

In this chapter, we will explore the vast world of **online business ventures** as a dynamic and versatile approach to building your passive income empire. The internet has revolutionized the way business is conducted, opening up opportunities for individuals to create sustainable income streams without the need for a physical presence. Whether you aspire to start an e-commerce store, create membership sites, or develop software as a service (SaaS), this chapter will provide the guidance you need to embark on your online business journey.

The Digital Economy: An Opportunity for All

The rise of the digital economy has democratized entrepreneurship. With access to the internet and the right skills and strategies, virtually anyone can create and grow an online business. Here's why online business ventures are a vital part of your passive income strategy:

1. Scalability

- Online businesses can scale rapidly with the potential to reach a global audience, creating significant income potential.

2. Low Overhead

- Many online businesses have low operational costs, making them accessible even to individuals with limited capital.

3. Flexibility

- Online businesses offer flexibility in terms of when and where you work, allowing you to tailor your work-life balance to your preferences.

4. Diverse Income Streams

- Online business models can generate income through various channels, such as advertising, product sales, memberships, and affiliate marketing.

Online Business Models for Passive Income

The digital landscape offers a plethora of online business models. Here are some popular options:

1. Dropshipping and E-commerce

- Create an e-commerce store and sell products to a global audience without holding inventory. Use dropshipping to fulfill orders.

2. Membership Sites and Subscription Services

- Develop a membership site or subscription service offering exclusive content, courses, or community access in exchange for recurring payments.

3. Software as a Service (SaaS)

- Create a software application or tool that solves a specific problem and charge users on a subscription basis.

4. Affiliate Marketing

- Promote other companies' products or services through your website or content. Earn commissions for each sale or lead generated.

5. Content Monetization

- Generate income through content creation on platforms like YouTube, blogs, podcasts, or social media. Monetize through ads, sponsorships, or merchandise sales.

6. Online Marketplaces

- Create a niche-focused online marketplace where buyers and sellers can transact, earning a commission on each sale.

Starting Your Online Business

Starting an online business requires careful planning and execution. Here are the steps to get you started:

1. Niche Selection

- Identify a niche or industry that aligns with your interests, expertise, and market demand.

2. Market Research

- Conduct thorough market research to understand your target audience, competition, and potential for profitability.

3. Business Model Selection

- Choose the online business model that best suits your niche and business goals.

4. Business Plan

- Develop a detailed business plan outlining your business strategy, revenue model, marketing plan, and financial projections.

5. Domain and Website

- Register a domain name and set up a professional website or e-commerce platform.

6. Content and Marketing

- Create high-quality content that attracts and engages your target audience. Implement effective digital marketing strategies.

7. Monetization

- Implement monetization strategies such as ads, product sales, affiliate marketing, or subscription models.

8. Customer Service

- Provide exceptional customer service to build trust and retain customers.

9. Analytics and Optimization

- Use data analytics to track performance and make data-driven decisions to optimize your business.

Scaling Your Online Business

Once your online business is up and running, the next step is scaling for growth. Consider these strategies:

1. Content Scaling

- Expand your content library to attract a larger audience and increase revenue through ads, sponsorships, and affiliate marketing.

2. Product Expansion

- Diversify your product offerings or develop complementary products to generate additional revenue streams.

3. Audience Engagement

- Focus on building a loyal audience through community engagement, email marketing, and social media.

4. Marketing Efforts

- Invest in targeted marketing campaigns to reach a broader audience and acquire new customers.

5. Outsourcing and Automation

- Delegate tasks and automate processes to free up your time for strategic growth efforts.

6. Partnerships and Collaborations

- Collaborate with other businesses or influencers in your niche to expand your reach and tap into new markets.

Risks and Considerations

While online business ventures offer substantial potential, they also come with risks and challenges:

1. **Competition**

- The digital landscape is highly competitive. To succeed, you must differentiate your business and provide unique value.

2. **Changing Trends**

- Online trends can evolve rapidly. Stay informed and adaptable to remain relevant.

3. **Security**

- Protect your online business against cyber threats and data breaches.

4. **Monetization Challenges**

- Monetizing your online business may take time. Be prepared for initial periods with lower income.

Conclusion

Online business ventures are a dynamic and accessible way to build your passive income empire in the digital age. By selecting the right niche, creating high-quality content or products, and implementing effective marketing strategies, you can create a sustainable income stream that provides flexibility and scalability. In the following chapters, we'll continue to explore additional passive income strategies, helping you diversify and strengthen your empire. Your digital journey to financial

independence awaits.

Chapter 8

Peer-to-Peer Lending - A Unique Approach to Passive Income

Introduction

Peer-to-peer (P2P) lending is a modern financial innovation that enables individuals to lend money directly to other individuals or small businesses. It offers a unique way to generate passive income by earning interest on loans you provide to borrowers. In this chapter, we will explore the world of P2P lending, its advantages, risks, and strategies for building a passive income stream through this platform.

The Rise of Peer-to-Peer Lending

P2P lending has gained popularity in recent years due to several factors:

1. Digital Accessibility

- Online platforms connect lenders and borrowers, making it easy to participate from anywhere with an internet connection.

2. Diverse Loan Types

- P2P platforms offer a wide range of loan types, from personal loans and small business loans to real estate crowdfunding and more.

3. Competitive Returns

- P2P lending often provides attractive interest rates for lenders, potentially outpacing traditional savings accounts and bonds.

4. Portfolio Diversification

- P2P lending allows investors to diversify their portfolios by allocating funds to various loans and risk profiles.

How Peer-to-Peer Lending Works

The process of P2P lending typically involves the following steps:

1. Registration

- Lenders and borrowers register on a P2P lending platform, providing necessary information and undergoing identity verification.

2. Loan Application

- Borrowers submit loan applications, specifying loan amount, purpose, and interest rate they are willing to pay.

3. Credit Evaluation

- P2P platforms assess borrowers' creditworthiness using credit reports, financial statements, and other relevant data.

4. Loan Listing

- Approved loan requests are listed on the platform for lenders to review.

5. Lender Selection

- Lenders select loans they want to fund based on borrower profiles, interest rates, and risk assessments.

6. Funding

- Lenders contribute funds to partially or fully fund the loan, spreading risk among multiple lenders.

7. Loan Repayment

- Borrowers make regular payments, including principal and interest, which are distributed to lenders.

8. Returns

- Lenders earn interest income from borrower repayments, generating passive income.

Advantages of Peer-to-Peer Lending

Investing in P2P lending offers several advantages for those seeking passive income:

1. Regular Cash Flow

- P2P lending provides a steady stream of income as borrowers make monthly payments.

2. Diversification

- Investors can spread their funds across various loans to reduce risk.

3. Attractive Returns

- P2P lending can yield higher returns compared to traditional savings accounts and some investments.

4. Transparency

- P2P platforms typically provide detailed borrower information and risk assessments, allowing lenders to make informed decisions.

Risks and Considerations

While P2P lending offers compelling benefits, it also comes with risks that lenders should be aware of:

1. Credit Risk

- There is a risk of borrowers defaulting on their loans, leading to potential loss of principal.

2. Platform Risk

- The platform itself may face financial difficulties or regulatory issues that impact lenders' ability to receive repayments.

3. Liquidity Risk

- P2P loans may have limited liquidity, making it challenging to sell loans if needed.

4. Diversification Challenges

- Diversification can be challenging, especially for lenders with limited capital, potentially increasing risk.

Building a P2P Lending Portfolio

To create a robust P2P lending portfolio, consider the following strategies:

1. Diversify

- Allocate your funds across a variety of loans to reduce credit risk. Spread your investments across different loan terms, purposes, and risk ratings.

2. Risk Assessment

- Carefully assess borrowers' credit profiles and loan purposes before lending.

3. Auto-Investing

- Utilize auto-investing tools offered by P2P platforms to automate loan selection and maintain a diversified portfolio.

4. **Reinvestment**

- Reinvest earned interest and principal repayments into new loans to maximize returns.

Tax Considerations

P2P lending income may be subject to taxes, depending on your country's tax laws. It's essential to understand the tax implications and report your earnings accurately.

Conclusion

Peer-to-peer lending provides a unique and accessible way to generate passive income by lending money directly to individuals and small businesses. While it offers attractive returns and diversification opportunities, it also comes with risks, primarily related to borrower default. By carefully assessing loans, diversifying your portfolio, and managing risk, you can build a reliable source of passive income through P2P lending. In the next chapters, we'll explore additional passive income strategies, helping you diversify and strengthen your empire. Your journey to financial independence continues with the possibilities of P2P lending.

Chapter 9

Realizing the Potential of Dividend Growth Investing

Introduction

Dividend growth investing is a powerful strategy for building a passive income empire. It involves investing in stocks of companies that not only pay dividends but also have a history of consistently increasing those dividends over time. In this chapter, we will explore the concept of dividend growth investing, its benefits, how to get started, and key strategies to maximize your dividend income and wealth.

The Essence of Dividend Growth Investing

Dividend growth investing focuses on building a portfolio of stocks from companies that not only pay dividends but also demonstrate a commitment to increasing those dividends year after year. The core principles of this strategy include:

1. Income Generation

- Dividend growth investors prioritize generating a steady stream of passive income from their investments.

2. Capital Appreciation

- Over time, companies that consistently increase their dividends tend to experience stock price appreciation, leading to capital gains for investors.

3. Long-Term Perspective

- Dividend growth investing is a long-term strategy that emphasizes the benefits of compounding and the snowball effect of increasing dividends.

Benefits of Dividend Growth Investing

Dividend growth investing offers several compelling advantages:

1. Steady and Increasing Income

- Companies that grow their dividends provide a reliable source of income that keeps pace with inflation.

2. Capital Preservation

- Dividend-paying stocks often exhibit more stability during market downturns, helping to protect capital.

3. Wealth Accumulation

- The combination of dividend income and capital appreciation can lead to significant wealth accumulation over time.

4. Passive Income

- Dividend growth investing aligns with the goal of building a passive income empire, where money works for you.

Building a Dividend Growth Portfolio

Creating a successful dividend growth portfolio involves several key steps:

1. **Research and Selection**

- Identify companies with a history of consistent dividend growth. Look for companies with competitive advantages and strong financials.

2. **Diversification**

- Diversify your portfolio across various sectors and industries to reduce risk. Avoid overconcentration in a single stock or sector.

3. **Dividend Yield vs. Growth**

- Balance your portfolio between higher-yield stocks and those with greater growth potential.

4. **Dividend Reinvestment**

- Consider enrolling in a dividend reinvestment plan (DRIP) to automatically reinvest your dividends into additional shares.

5. **Regular Monitoring**

- Keep a watchful eye on your portfolio, evaluating the performance of your holdings and making adjustments as needed.

Strategies for Maximizing Dividend Income

To maximize your dividend income, consider these strategies:

1. **Dividend Aristocrats and Champions**

- These are companies with a history of consistently increasing dividends for 25 or more years. They are often reliable choices for long-term dividend growth.

2. **Dividend Reinvestment**

- Reinvesting your dividends allows you to benefit from the compounding effect and accelerate your wealth accumulation.

3. **Selective Selling**

- Occasionally, it may make sense to trim positions in stocks that have become overvalued or no longer align with your investment goals.

4. **Tax Efficiency**

- Consider holding dividend-paying stocks in tax-advantaged accounts like IRAs to minimize the tax impact of your dividend income.

5. Regular Contributions

- Consistently add new funds to your dividend growth portfolio to take advantage of dollar-cost averaging and purchase shares at different price points.

Risks and Considerations

While dividend growth investing is generally considered a low-risk strategy, it's essential to be aware of potential risks:

1. Market Volatility

- Dividend-paying stocks are not immune to market fluctuations. Be prepared for periods of price volatility.

2. Dividend Cuts

- While rare among dividend aristocrats, some companies may reduce or eliminate dividends during challenging economic times.

3. Company-Specific Risks

- Conduct thorough research to assess the financial health and prospects of the companies in your portfolio.

Conclusion

Dividend growth investing is a time-tested strategy for building a passive income empire and accumulating wealth over time. By carefully selecting dividend growth stocks, diversifying your portfolio, and implementing smart investment strategies, you can harness the power of dividends to achieve your financial goals. In the next chapters, we'll continue to explore additional passive income strategies, helping you diversify and strengthen your empire. Your journey to financial independence continues with the potential of dividend growth investing.

Chapter 10:

The Art of Rental Properties - Unlocking Real Estate Passive Income

Introduction

Rental properties have long been celebrated as a tried-and-true method for generating passive income and building wealth. In this chapter, we will delve deep into the world of **rental properties** and explore the strategies, benefits, risks, and essential steps to create a thriving real estate portfolio that contributes to your passive income empire.

The Allure of Rental Properties

Rental properties hold enduring appeal for income seekers and investors for several compelling reasons:

1. Steady Income Stream

- Rental properties provide a consistent and reliable income stream, often paid monthly by tenants.

2. Wealth Accumulation

- Real estate properties tend to appreciate in value over time, contributing to long-term wealth accumulation.

3. Tax Advantages

- Rental property owners enjoy various tax benefits, including deductions for mortgage interest, property taxes, and depreciation.

4. Portfolio Diversification

- Real estate investments can diversify your overall investment portfolio, helping to spread risk.

Strategies for Rental Property Success

To build a successful portfolio of rental properties, you need a well-thought-out strategy:

1. Property Selection

- Choose properties that align with your budget, location preferences, and investment goals. Consider factors like property type (single-family, multi-family, commercial), location, and potential for appreciation.

2. Financing

- Secure financing through mortgages or alternative lending options. Analyze interest rates, loan terms, and down payment requirements to find the best fit for your financial situation.

3. Property Management

- Decide whether you will manage the property yourself or hire a property management company. Property management involves tasks like tenant screening, maintenance, rent collection, and addressing tenant issues.

4. Tenant Screening

- Implement a rigorous tenant screening process to find reliable tenants who pay rent on time and take good care of the property. Background checks, credit checks, and rental history assessments are essential.

5. Property Maintenance

- Regularly maintain the property to keep it in good condition. A well-maintained property can attract and retain tenants while preserving property value.

6. Legal and Tax Considerations

- Consult with legal and tax professionals to understand local laws, landlord-tenant regulations, and tax implications for rental income.

7. Insurance

- Purchase landlord insurance to protect your property and income in case of unexpected events, such as property damage or liability claims.

Scaling Your Rental Property Portfolio

As your rental property portfolio grows, consider these strategies for scaling your investments:

1. Additional Acquisitions

- Purchase more rental properties as your financial situation allows. Expanding your portfolio can significantly increase your passive income.

2. Renovations and Improvements

- Increase the value of existing properties by making strategic renovations and improvements that can justify higher rent.

3. Optimization

- Continuously optimize your portfolio by assessing property performance and making necessary adjustments. Consider selling underperforming properties and reinvesting in better opportunities.

4. Market Expansion

- Explore opportunities in different geographic areas to diversify your property holdings and mitigate risks associated with local market fluctuations.

Risks and Considerations

While rental properties offer tremendous potential for passive income, they are not without risks and considerations:

1. Vacancy Risk

- Extended vacancies can impact your rental income and cash flow. It's crucial to have a plan for handling vacancies and attracting new tenants.

2. Maintenance Costs

- Property maintenance and repairs can be costly. Budget for ongoing maintenance and unexpected repairs to avoid financial strain.

3. Tenant Issues

- Dealing with difficult tenants, late payments, and legal disputes can be challenging. Establish clear rental agreements and tenant communication channels to address issues promptly.

4. Market Volatility

- Real estate markets can experience fluctuations in property values and rental rates. Be prepared for market changes and have strategies in place to adapt.

Conclusion

Rental properties are a potent avenue for generating passive income and building wealth over time. By carefully selecting properties, managing them effectively, and scaling your portfolio strategically, you can create a reliable and growing stream of rental income. In the next chapters, we'll explore additional passive income strategies, helping you diversify and strengthen your empire. Your journey to financial independence continues with the potential of rental properties.

Conclusion: Building Your Passive Income Empire

Congratulations! You've reached the conclusion of "The Ultimate Guide to Building a Passive Income Empire." Throughout this comprehensive guide, we've explored a wide array of passive income strategies, each offering its unique advantages and opportunities for wealth creation. Let's recap the key takeaways and insights to help you on your journey to financial independence:

1. **Diverse Income Streams**: Building a passive income empire is all about diversifying your income sources. By leveraging various strategies, you reduce risk and enhance your financial stability.

2. **Real Estate**: Real estate investments, including rental properties, REITs, and crowdfunding, offer steady cash flow, appreciation potential, and tax advantages. Proper research, property management, and diversification are critical to success.

3. **Dividend Growth Investing**: Dividend stocks from companies with a history of consistent dividend growth provide regular income, capital appreciation, and wealth accumulation. Careful stock selection and diversification are key.

4. **Online Business Ventures**: The digital economy provides opportunities for e-commerce, membership sites, software as a service, and more. Online businesses offer scalability, flexibility, and diverse income streams.

5. **Peer-to-Peer Lending**: P2P lending can generate interest income, but it comes with credit and platform risks. Diversify your loans, monitor your portfolio, and be aware of potential defaults.

6. **Passive Income Mindset**: Developing a passive income empire requires patience, discipline, and a long-term perspective. Continuously educate yourself, adapt to changing circumstances, and stay focused on your financial goals.

7. **Risk Management**: Every passive income strategy comes with risks. It's crucial to understand these risks, conduct thorough due diligence, and have contingency plans in place.

8. **Regular Monitoring and Adjustment**: Passive income strategies require ongoing monitoring and adjustments. Review your investments, track performance, and make necessary changes to optimize your income.

9. **Tax Efficiency**: Explore tax-advantaged accounts and strategies to minimize the tax impact of your passive income, allowing you to keep more of what you earn.

10. **Consistent Effort**: Building a passive income empire is not entirely hands-off. While it can provide financial freedom, it requires initial effort and ongoing management.

Remember, your journey to financial independence is unique, and your passive income empire can be tailored to align with your goals, risk tolerance, and interests. As you continue on this path, remain committed to your financial well-being and stay open to new opportunities and strategies that may arise.

The knowledge and strategies you've gained in this guide are powerful tools for achieving financial freedom. Embrace the possibilities, stay informed, and take proactive steps toward building and strengthening your passive income empire. Your financial independence is within reach, and with dedication and smart choices, you can turn your dreams into reality.

Keep building, keep growing, and watch your passive income empire thrive.

www.ingramcontent.com/pod-product-compliance
Lightning Source LLC
Chambersburg PA
CBHW062250290526
45794CB00006B/2485